MR. LUMBERJACK

Story by Rick Bergh
Music by Erica Phare-Bergh
Artwork by
Franceska Dnestrianschii

Mr. Lumberjack
Copyright © 2015 by R.E.Bergh Consulting Inc.

Find the *5-BIG Words*:
swath | culprit | sawdust | sneered | insisted

For the FREE sing-a-long song and FREE *5-BIG Words* learning page, please go to www.asongwitheverystory.com/mrlumberjack/

Also available online for purchase is a <u>Music Educator's Package</u> that includes:
♫ **Original song back-up track**
♫ **Song chart**
♫ **Classical composer worksheet (excerpt hidden within each song)**
♫ **Lesson plan**

  Go to: www.asongwitheverystory.com/mrlumberjack/teacher/

Published by 🌲 **BEACON MOUNT** P U B L I S H I N G

18 West Chapman Place, Cochrane, Alberta, T4C 1J9, Canada.
www.asongwitheverystory.com

ISBN 978-0-9947962-5-7 (Paperback)
ISBN 978-1-988082-15-8 (Hardcover)
ISBN 978-0-9947962-8-8 (ePub)
ISBN 978-1-988082-12-7 (Mobi)

Printed in the United States of America

Dedicated to all my children,
Devon, Keeara, Larissa, and Landon,
who as kids loved hearing this story and singing the song.

In a deep, thick forest, there lived a lumberjack who loved his life.
Each morning, he would walk out the front door of his cabin, look up at the sky, take a deep breath and sing:

My name is Mr. Lumberjack and I cut down trees, BIG TREES!

My name is Mr. Lumberjack and I cut down trees, BIG TREES!

7

One morning, he woke up, walked out the front door of his cabin, looked up at the sky, took a deep breath and...he was shocked!

OH NOOOO!!!

8

To his horror, he saw a huge swath of trees that had been cut down.
It went for miles and miles. The saddest part was that it wasn't ONLY big
trees that were lying on the ground, but medium trees, small trees and tiny trees too!

"This is disgusting! I wonder who made this mess," he said to himself. "This is not right!" And he sang:

My name is Mr. Lumberjack and I cut down trees, BIG TREES!

My name is Mr. Lumberjack and I cut down trees, BIG TREES!

My name is Mr. Lumberjack and I cut down trees, BIG TREES!

Mr. Lumberjack knew that it was not right to cut down tiny trees, small trees or even medium trees. "You only cut down BIG TREES!" he yelled into the forest.

BIG TREES ONLY!

He thought for a while. Then he decided that he should go and find the culprit.

He grabbed his backpack; made himself an enormous lumberjack lunch; put on his heavy lumberjack boots; grabbed his huge lumberjack axe; and followed the path of fallen trees into the forest.

He climbed up big mountains.
He hiked down deep valleys.
He swam across wide rivers.
He swatted huge mosquitoes.

And he sang as he went:

My name is Mr. Lumberjack and I cut down trees, BIG TREES!

My name is Mr. Lumberjack and I cut down trees, BIG TREES!

15

It was a long and tiring journey, but Mr. Lumberjack did not give up.

The only time he stopped was to sleep.

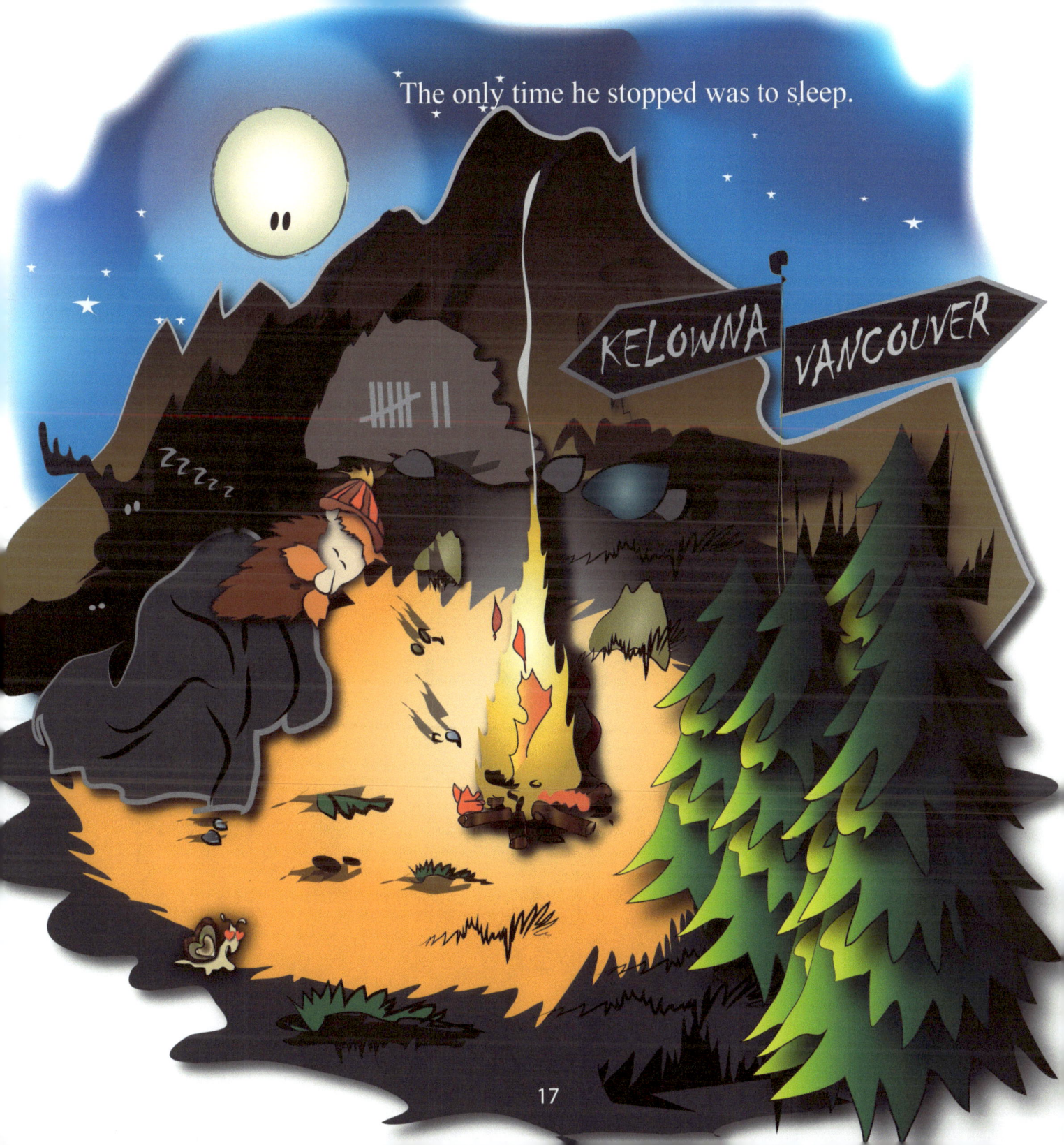

KELOWNA

VANCOUVER

After 21 days, 13 hours, 51 minutes and 4 seconds, he heard the sound of a big chainsaw.

He also heard the trees as they pleaded,
"Oh please, don't cut us down! We're too small and need to grow up!"
It was not a pretty sight - there was sawdust everywhere.

Oh please, don't cut us down!

At the end of the path of fallen trees, there was a man holding a chainsaw.
"Are you responsible for this mess?" asked Mr. Lumberjack.
"What mess are you talking about?" sneered the man, whose name was Mr. Weasel.

Mr. Lumberjack answered, "You can't cut down tiny trees, small trees or even medium trees in a forest!"

Mr. Weasel replied, "Who are *you* to tell me that I can't cut down trees?"

And Mr. Lumberjack began to sing his song:

My name is Mr. Lumberjack and I cut down trees, BIG TREES!

My name is Mr. Lumberjack and I cut down trees, BIG TREES!

My name is Mr. Lumberjack and I cut down trees, BIG TREES!

"I can cut down any tree in the forest that I want to!" said Mr. Weasel.

"No, you can't!" Mr. Lumberjack insisted.

"You need to wait for them to grow up first," said Mr. Lumberjack.
"Yeah? What are going to do about it?" said Mr. Weasel.

24

And then, to Mr. Weasel's surprise, Mr. Lumberjack picked him up and, with all his might, threw him into the middle of the ocean.

All the trees clapped and cheered. And Mr. Lumberjack just smiled and sang:

CLAP!

CLAP!

CLAP!

My name is Mr. Lumberjack and I cut down trees, BIG TREES!

My name is Mr. Lumberjack and I cut down trees, BIG TREES!

My name is Mr. Lumberjack and I cut down trees, BIG TREES!

27

Would you like to know what happened to Mr. Weasel after he was thrown into the ocean?
He became a fisherman.

And do you know what kind of fish he caught?

...BIG FISH!!

Mr. Lumberjack

Words and music by Erica Phare-Bergh

My name is Mr. Lumberjack and I cut down trees, BIG TREES!
My name is Mr. Lumberjack and I cut down trees, BIG TREES!
I'm a keeper of the forest, a protector of the trees
I'm a friend to all the animals - the foxes, bears and bees
My name is Mr. Lumberjack and I cut down trees, BIG TREES!

Left! Right! Left, right, left!
Right! Left! Right, left, right!

My name is Mr. Lumberjack and I cut down trees, BIG TREES!
My name is Mr. Lumberjack and I cut down trees, BIG TREES!
And when a person cuts down baby trees that haven't grown
It makes me sad because these little trees were barely sown
My name is Mr. Lumberjack and I cut down trees, BIG TREES!

Left! Right! Left, right, left!
Right! Left! Right, left, right!

Interlude:
"Hall of the Mountain King" *(Peer Gynt Suite)* by Edvard Grieg

My name is Mr. Lumberjack and I cut down trees, BIG TREES!
My name is Mr. Lumberjack and I cut down trees, BIG TREES!
And so I try to show someone who doesn't understand
That forests need our help and are the future of our land
My name is Mr. Lumberjack and I cut down trees, BIG TREES!

I am the keeper - the manager of green
I am the ranger - the forest's lean machine
I'm Mr. Lumberjack!!!

Also available in the *A Song with Every Story* series

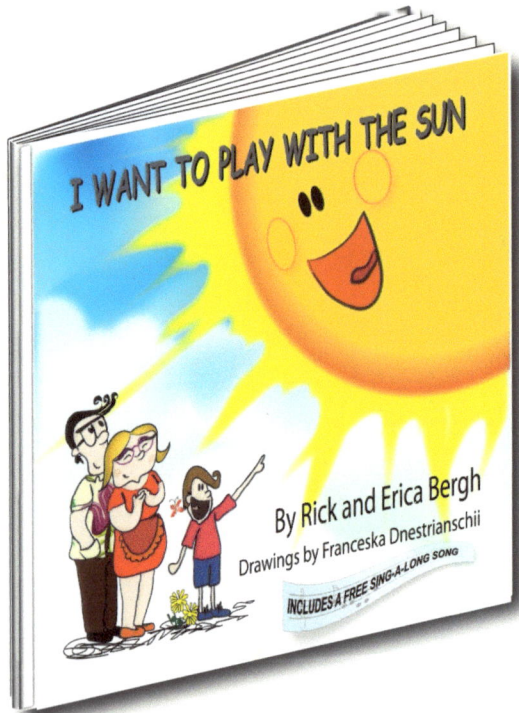

I Want to Play with the Sun

Devon wanted to play with the sun. Little did he know the disruption it would cause in his entire town when he reached up and grabbed it out of the sky.

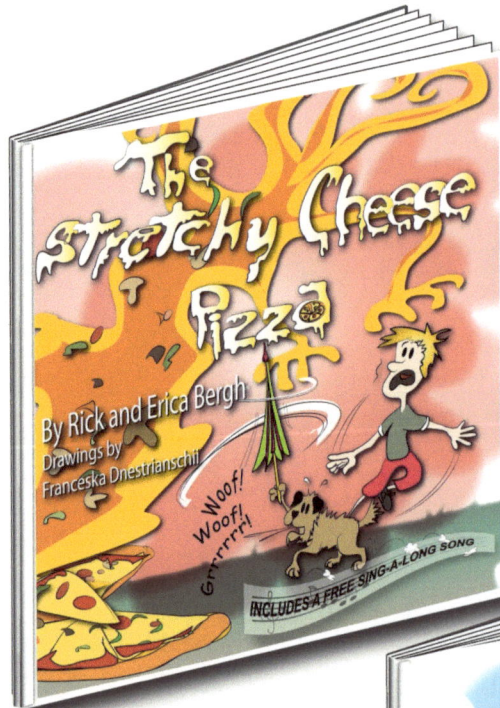

The Stretchy Cheese Pizza

Connor's mom invites him to make his very own pizza, but he soon discovers that the mound of cheese that he put on top has a mind of its own....

I Want to Grow a Beard

Connor wants to grow up too quickly and be just like his dad. His dream comes true the next morning when he wakes up with a full beard. But he soon discovers that being an adult isn't all that it's cracked up to be.

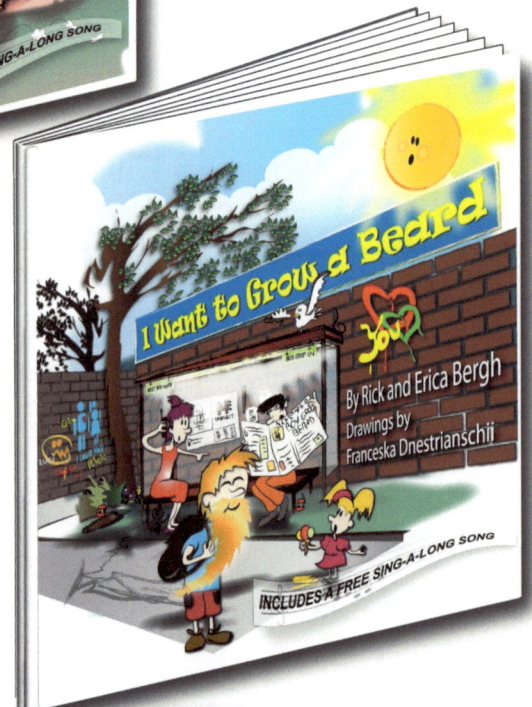

Please check out our books at *www.asongwitheverystory.com*